A MEASURED PACE

WILLIAM L. COLEMAN

A MEASURED PACE

BETHANY HOUSE PUBLISHERS
MINNEAPOLIS, MINNESOTA 55438

MEASURED PACE

Published by Bethany House Publishers
A Division of Bethany Fellowship, Inc.
6820 Auto Club Road, Minneapolis, MN 55438

Printed in the United States of America

Library of Congress Cataloging-in-Publication Data

Coleman, William L.
    A measured pace.

    1. Meditations.   I. Title.
BV4832.2.C593   1986   242   86-11750
ISBN 0-87123-671-0

WILLIAM L. COLEMAN

is the well-known author of nearly three dozen books on a wide variety of topics. Combining his vast experience as a pastor, researcher, writer and speaker, Bill is noted for his effective communication in the area of family relationships and practical spiritual growth. He has been married for over twenty years and is the father of three children.

CONTENTS

CONTENTS

THE PAUSE BUTTON

Reflection is a noble word. It means once in a while we stop life and think it over. Where are we going and why? How can we check our bearings and make sure this is the course we want to follow?

Pause to laugh, to wonder, to dream, to weigh, to ask, to hope, and talk to God. Sit still and consider what is really delicious in life. What satisfies over and over again.

Naturally there are surprises in reflecting. We might get to know God better and find out we really like each other.

Bill Coleman
Aurora, Nebraska

IN AN OPEN FIELD

I wish I could meet Jesus / In an open field,
Without pews or organs, / Without covered dishes
Or bulletins to map out / My life.

To meet Jesus one on one. / To hear Him speak.
To pick up His tone. / To see the texture / Of His smile.

To meet the man / Woven with the Divine.

In an open field
I'll take Him as He comes.
I'll see His firmness
And I truly believe
I will feel how
Much He cares.

I have heard how much,
I have read how much,
I have discussed how much.
But then I will feel
How much He cares.

And in that moment
With nothing in my hand,
Without title, credentials,
Or prepared remarks,
I will feel accepted
By the Son of God.

And I will know
It's all right.

My mistakes aren't important.
My inabilities don't matter.
My inconsistencies are overlooked.
And my sins
Are forgiven and forgotten.

Because only Jesus could
Make everything all right.

In that moment
In an open field,
I will feel what
It is like to be
With Jesus.

And it's all right.

℘

"He wanted to see who Jesus was."
Luke 19:3, NIV

MAKING DEPOSITS

It's a perfect day
To make deposits
In other people's accounts.

They won't be expecting it.
It will seem like a gift
From heaven,
And it will be.

Maybe we will touch
Someone with kindness
And bring a smile
To his life.

Or put a flower
On someone's desk
And not tell her
Who did it.

We will make deposits
In their accounts.
And they will be richer
Because we passed by.

Maybe we will drop
A card in the mail
Or make a quick call
Just to brighten
Their day.

It's the work of God
To make deposits
In other people's accounts.
Not His only work,
But the work of God.

℘

"I tell you the truth, anyone who gives you
a cup of water in my name because you belong
to Christ will certainly not lose his reward."
Mark 9:41, NIV

15

WHY DO I FEAR?

Why am I afraid?
Afraid of change,
Afraid of loss,
Afraid of people.

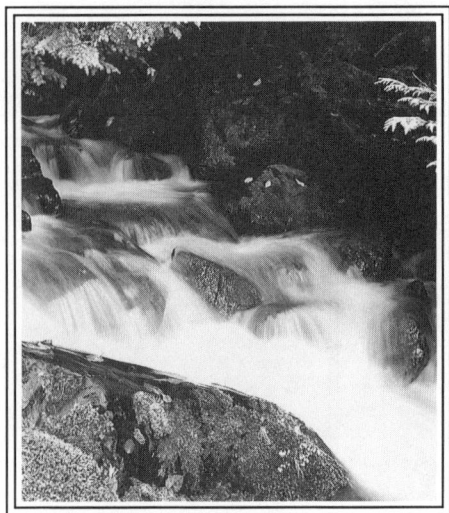

Like a steady stream
It runs beneath the surface —
Constant, rolling,
Always there.
A quiet fear that
Seldom goes away.

Why am I afraid?
Afraid of myself,
Afraid of God,
Afraid of those
Who love me.

Why do I keep
My guard up,
Taking no chances
Lest I open up
And get hurt?

Confused, I hide
The real me,
Stalking in the dense jungle,
Ready to pounce if
Anyone gets too close.

Help me love others.
Help me love God.
Help me love myself.

Why do I keep
My guard up,
Taking no chances
Lest I open up
And get hurt?

Help me to love.
Help me to trust.
Help me to believe.

Help me to rest
In the arms
Of a God who
Loves me.

&

"There is no fear in love."
1 John 4:18, NIV

LIKE A CHILD

Do you ever have
The feeling
That life is going
The wrong way?

That we work hard
To become
What we really don't
Want to be?

With dedication
We create ulcers,
Accumulate debt,
Attract pain
As if it were
Expensive perfume.

And when we are
Locked in,
Shackled and
Miserable,
We call it
Adulthood.

Do you ever have
The feeling
That life is going
The wrong way?

Do you ever long
For the simple joy
Of being a child
Again?

When you were thrilled
With ice cream
On a stick.

When an evening out
Meant chasing fireflies
In the backyard.

When it felt good
To squeeze mud
Through your toes.

And you thought
A yo-yo was
A technological wonder.

When you found it easy
To believe in God
And miracles
And heaven
And angels.

Not because you heard an
Amazing speaker,
But because you felt it
In your heart.

Do you ever have
The feeling
That life is going
The wrong way?

Maybe we need
To become
Children again.

&

"And he said: 'I tell you the truth,
unless you change and become like little children,
you will never enter the kingdom of heaven.'"
Matthew 18:3, NIV

YESTERDAY

I could live in yesterday
And pamper my regrets.
I could wonder why
I didn't take this road
Or why I didn't take
Another turn.

I could live in yesterday
And pretend it was more
Wonderful and happy
Than it really was.

I could live in fantasies
And pretend I was
A hero, a leader,
A charmer, a neat person
Whom everyone quietly envied.

I could rearrange my yesterdays
Like furniture
Or socks in a drawer.

Yesterday was a friend,
But a friend that must
Let go.
Yesterday was a party,
But a party that has
To end.

I kiss it goodbye.
I bid it farewell.
Thanks for the memories,
But you have to go
Now.

Today calls
And today is magnificent.
Today calls
And today is vibrant.
Today calls
And today bubbles over
With opportunity.

Thanks, yesterday,
But I have to go.
Today is too rich
To miss.

&

"But I press on to take hold of that
for which Christ Jesus took hold of me."
Philippians 3:12, NIV

FEELING GOOD

It feels good
To be alive today.

You can feel the contentment
Down to your toes.

The coffee tastes good,
Your clothes fit well,
Even the air seems fresh
In your lungs.

There is no hiding the fact.
There is no need to feel
Guilty about it.

God has created a good day
And it's all yours.
Like a round red apple
Waiting to be eaten —
Chewed, savored, and enjoyed.

Life has more than its share
Of hard days
And bitter pills to swallow.

No need to dwell on them.
No need to fear them.
No need to be suspicious.

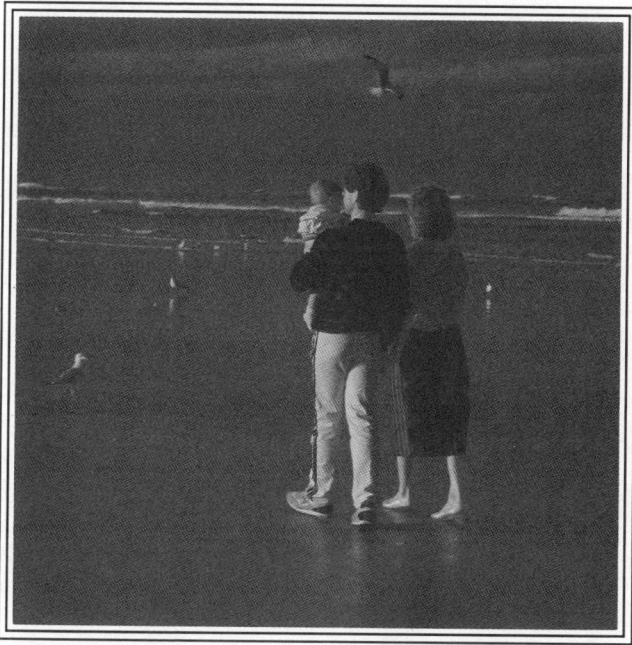

Today is good.
Don't chase it away / Or pretend it / Isn't real.

Today is beautiful, / Created by a loving God.
Drink it in, / Use it wisely, And thank God / For it.

&

A RUNAWAY TRAIN

We all get the feeling
That things are
Out of control.

As if we were in
A mad rush
To nowhere.

We are accelerating
Like a runaway train.

Job, school, church,
Committees, ballgames,
Seminars, appointments,
Each carrying us
Downhill,
Rapidly picking up
Speed.

You can feel the panic
Start to set in.
The adrenaline flows
As you watch
Trees blur as
You go by.

God, help me
Find the brake
Before I crash.

Show me how
To slow down
To a manageable
Speed.

Help me regain
The controls
Of my runaway train.

I need to breathe
Easily again.
I need to hear
My children laugh again.
I need to dwell
With God again
In a measured pace.

Let's slow down
And get to know
Each other again.

❦

"It is better to have self-control
than to control an army."
Proverbs 16:32, TLB

I FEEL LIKE SHOUTING

It doesn't happen every day;

But some days you want to

Stand on your desk

And shout for joy.

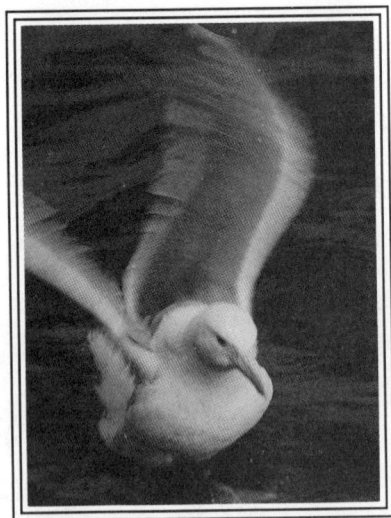

How good can life get?

Have you ever walked
Down the street and
Wanted to leap in the
Air?

Naturally, you're too dignified.
It wouldn't be good
For your image.
And, besides,
You might twist your
Ankle.

But inside you're leaping
And hopping
And throwing your hands
High.

You want to shout
At the top of your voice,
"Thank God!"

But, naturally you're too
Dignified.

You restrain yourself,
Straighten your clothes,
And comb your hair.

You think
Dignified people
Don't shout for joy
Even when their hearts
Are overflowing.

&

"Shout for joy before the Lord."
Psalm 98:6, NIV

HELP ME DREAM!

Help me put my faith
To work.
Help me open up my mind
And dare
To dream.

Help me see things
I never imagined.
Help me feel things
I have never known.

Never let me settle again
For a dull life,
For a stodgy routine,
For a monotonous life
That reeks of the smell
Of dust.

Help me dream of things
That only God could do.
Help my mind see
New visions and new hopes
Of what could be done
If I would put my faith
To work.

Save me from drowning
In security.
Protect me from the ruts
Of boredom.
Rescue me from the walls
Of hopelessness.

What new adventures
Are waiting to be
Accomplished?
What can I do that
I have been afraid
To try?

Open my soul
And let my faith
Pour out
To try new things.

In reaching for dreams
I walk with God,
For God is the Dreamer
Who continues to create.

&

"Now faith is being sure of what we
hope for and certain of what we do not see."
Hebrews 11:1, NIV

HE SEES OUR TEARS

We don't cry very often.
But every now and then
The tears find a way.

It's cool to be brave
And stand above
Our emotions,
But sometimes they are
Too much
To be denied.

We don't want to show
Too much happiness
Lest we get carried away.

We don't want to show
Too much sadness
Lest we lose control.

Keep it in.
Be the master.
Show just how
Stoic and placid
We can be.

We don't cry very often.
But every now and then
The tears find a way.

Then we are glad to know
That God stands close by.
He may not speak,
He may not act,
But it is enough to know
That God stands close by.

He sees us cry,
And just His presence
Makes us feel better.

We are not alone.
We are never abandoned.
Like a strong friend,
God stands near.
He listens, He understands,
And sometimes God
Weeps with us.

&

"I have heard your prayer
and seen your tears."
2 Kings 20:5, NIV

HOLDING ON

What do we do when
We are too weak to
Hold on?

What do we do when
Strength, hope, and courage
Have died?

When we think we will
Never win again?
When we can't find
A reason to go on?

When we have lost
All direction,
Form,
Cohesion,
Purpose?

When we can no longer
Think in a straight line
Or clear our minds
Well enough to reason?

Then we reach beyond reason.
We grab hold of faith
And we hold on,
And we hold on.

And as we take firm grasp
Of Jesus Christ,
Jesus Christ
Takes hold of us.

He gives strength
When reason fails.
He gives hope
When every road is blocked.

From inside, Jesus
Furnishes spiritual strength
And the courage to
Go on.

❦

"I can do everything through him
who gives me strength."
Philippians 4:13, NIV

GOD GIVES LAUGHTER

Laughing from deep inside
Until your stomach jiggles,
Your eyes water,
And your sides ache.

Laughing with children,
Rolling on the floor,
Or watching Bill Cosby
Make faces at his
Teenage son.

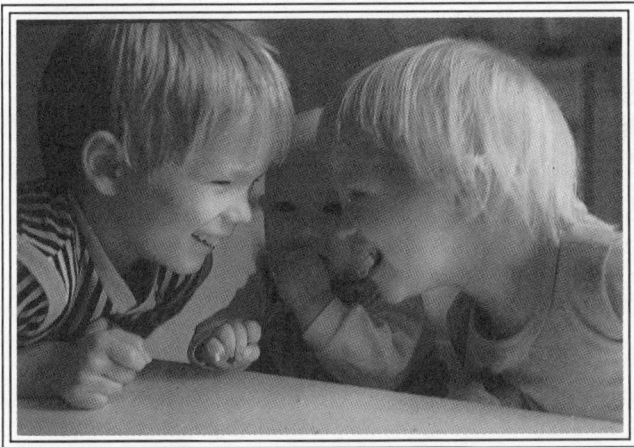

No longer distrusting laughter
As if it were a narcotic
Or an invention of Satan
Himself.

Letting go to welcome
Happiness
Without fear, hesitation,
Or embarrassment.

Laughing at your socks
That don't match.
Laughing at the keys
You misplaced.
Laughing at the gray
Inching across your hair.
Laughing at the cake
That sank.

Receiving laughter as
A medicine —
Mixed, bottled and
Delivered
Directly by God.

We laugh because
Life is peculiar.
We laugh because
Joy is free.
We laugh because
God is alive.

And God laughs
With us.

&

"Our mouths were filled with laughter,
  our tongues with songs of joy.
  Then it was said among the nations,
  'The Lord has done great things for them.'"

Psalm 126:2, NIV

SOMETIMES I WONDER

Most days I feel confident
In what I believe;
And my faith stands straight
Like a well-trimmed soldier.

But once in a while
I wonder
What is really going on.

Questions come like
A headache on a bad day.
Doubts start to rise up like
A cowlick
On a well-groomed head.

I used to hate doubt
As if it were an enemy,
And I asked God
To take it away and
Never let it return.

But doubts come back
Like gnats in the summer,
Or box elder bugs on
A basement carpet.

I no longer ask God
To slay my doubts,
For I have learned
To use them.

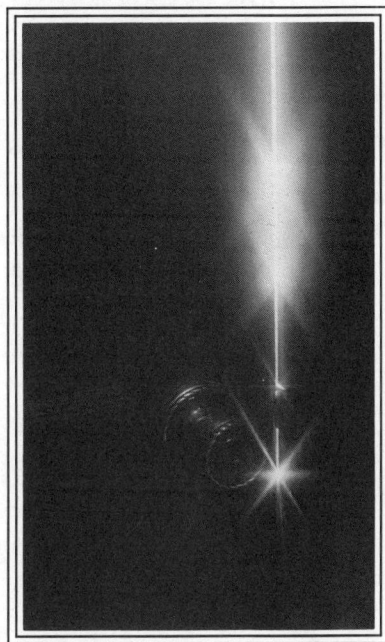

I have learned that
Questions are my friend,
That thinking is a sign
Of life,
That challenges are nutrients
Causing me to grow.

Now I ask God to
Keep me level,
To entertain questions,
But not to let them
Move in and take over.

If I am afraid to
Look doubts in the eye,
If I am threatened by
The invitation to wonder,
Then my faith is settled,
Determined, resolved, concrete —
And maybe dead.

My faith needs a brisk
Walk in the night.
My faith needs to be
Exposed to a cold wind
Now and then.

Sometimes I wonder
About the things
I believe.
And I find my faith
Stronger for it.

&

"Be merciful to those who doubt."
Jude 22, NIV

HAPPY WHERE I AM

When we were children, / We wanted to be
Firemen with shining helmets, / Riding trucks that screamed
As they dashed through the streets.

When we were young, / We wanted to race / Across the prairie
Atop a beautiful steed, / Hair stretched against the wind,
Chaps pressed tightly / Against the saddle.

When we were growing,
We wanted to challenge
The stars and beyond.
To don the astronaut suit,
Climb the stairs,
And roar into space.
To walk on planets,
To stare into craters,
And watch colored hues
Change on the horizon.

But we grew up
And our dreams moved around,
Slowly, deliberately,
Like slides on the wall.

Today our hopes are different.
We have found
The most important thing
To be.
I want to be me.

The me God made.
The me God molded.
The me God mended.
The me God mellowed.

I pull in my neck,
For I don't need
To watch others.

I pull in my eyes,
For I don't need
To envy.

I pull in my tongue,
For I don't need
To thirst
After things.

I want to be me.
Just the way
God made me.

℘

"A heart at peace gives life to the body,
  but envy rots the bones."
                                Proverbs 14:30, NIV

RUBBER DUCKS

When you were a kid,
You sat in the tub
With your little rubber duck,
And liked to push it to
The bottom.

If you wanted to, you could
Hold your duck for
A long time;
But when you let go,
It bounced back
To the top.

You held your rubber duck
For a while and then
You let it go.
And it popped back
To the top.

Rubber ducks are like that.
You can put them down,
You can even hold them down,
But you can't keep them down.

> Sooner or later they can always
> Bounce back up again.

Christians are like that.
You can put them down,
You can even hold them down,
But you can't keep them down.

> Sooner or later they can always
> Bounce back up again.

Jesus Christ furnishes the bounce
For the rubber-duck Christian.

&

"I am greatly encouraged;
 in all our troubles my joy knows no bounds."
                2 Corinthians 7:4, NIV

FEELING FORGIVEN

Some days it seems too easy.
How can forgiveness be free,
Open, generous, and kind?

I feel I must pay for what
I do wrong
And keep paying and paying.

Jesus tells me to go
And sin no more,
But I know better.
So I resist and keep
Trying to pay.

Guilt sits like a scab
On my hand.
I pick at it and keep
It open.
I pick at it and make
It bleed.
I fight against healing,
As if guilt were part
Of me
And I would hate to see
It leave.

Jesus is so good about it.
It's almost ridiculous.
He wants to set me free,
But I stay enslaved.
He wants to wash it clean,
But I want to keep it soiled.
He wants to forget it,
But I want it fresh
Like watered lettuce.

The fact is I am forgiven.
The trick is to get
My feelings to match
The facts.

Jesus has let go
Of my guilt.
Now I must let go,
Too.

&

"When Jesus saw their faith,
he said to the paralytic,
'Son, your sins are forgiven.'"
Mark 2:5, NIV

WOUNDS OF A FRIEND

Once in a while,
But not too often,
A friend will wound me.

Not out of meanness
Or because he likes
To hurt me.
Not carelessly or
Without thinking.

He wounds me because
He wants to help.

He dares to tell me
When I am wrong.
He dares to tell me
I need to change.

It's risky business because
It can backfire.
It can be misunderstood.
It can cause resentment.

A good friend does it
Carefully and gently,
But he knows it must be done.

Once in a while,
But not too often,
A friend will wound me.

And I will bleed,
And I will be stunned,
And I will be better off.

If I am to be hurt,
If I am to see myself
For what I really am,
Let it be at the hands
Of a good friend.

He hurts only when
He has to.
He hurts in order
To heal.
He never hurts for
The joy
Of seeing me in pain.

Once in a while,
But not too often,
A friend will wound me.

And I thank God
For a friend who
Cares that much.

&

"The kisses of an enemy may be profuse,
but faithful are the wounds of a friend."
Proverbs 27:6, NIV

FREEDOM

The cell door is open —

Not just a crack or

Slightly ajar.

It's wide open

Exactly as Jesus left it.

I'm free to go,

To walk out,

To roam around

Without tether or chain.

I'm free to live.
I'm free to love.
I'm free to serve.
I'm free to commune
With God
One on one.

But like a prisoner
Kept too long,
I am afraid.
Afraid of the light,
Afraid of the dignity
Which Jesus has given me.

People hold me prisoner.
They poke at me.
They jeer and intimidate.
They become my judges
And tell me to stay
Put.

They know what God
Wants for me.
They read their map
And tell me how
To travel.

But I cannot live
With Jesus Christ
By someone else's
Choices.

I must be free,
Though freedom scares
Me.

I must be open,
Though openness threatens
Me.

Jesus opened the door

And called me to walk

In the sunshine.

Others told me to stay

Put,

To play it safe.

I must risk freedom,

For only in freedom

Can I begin to walk

With Jesus Christ.

"It is for freedom that
  Christ has set us free."
                    Galatians 5:1, NIV

COLORING "E'S"

Sitting in a pew
With nothing to do
But color in the "E's"
In my bulletin.

Closing them tightly
With dark blue,
Then looking for the "O's"
And coloring them, too.

Wondering why something
Isn't said or done.
Hearing words that bounce
From wall to wall,
But never settling
On my heart or mind.

Insult me.
Accuse me.
Challenge me.
Surprise me.
Amuse me.
Dare me.
But please,
Please don't
Bore me.

Counting tiles
Lined on a ceiling,
Watching a box elder bug
Hiking across a pew.

Looking at a child
Curled in a ball
Sleeping peacefully
With a hymnal
For a pillow,
And wishing I could, too.

Sitting in a pew
With nothing to do
But color in the "E's"
In my bulletin.

&

"Seated in a window was a young man named Eutychus,
who was sinking into a deep sleep as Paul talked on
and on. When he was sound asleep, he fell to the ground
from the third story and was picked up dead."
Acts 20:9, NIV

GOD CLEANING UP

Can you picture God
Standing on a cliff
And tossing objects
Into the sea?
Picking up tiny pieces
And seeing how far
He can throw them.
Struggling with an occasional
Large object
And sending it
Tumbling down the side,
Plummeting into
The water.

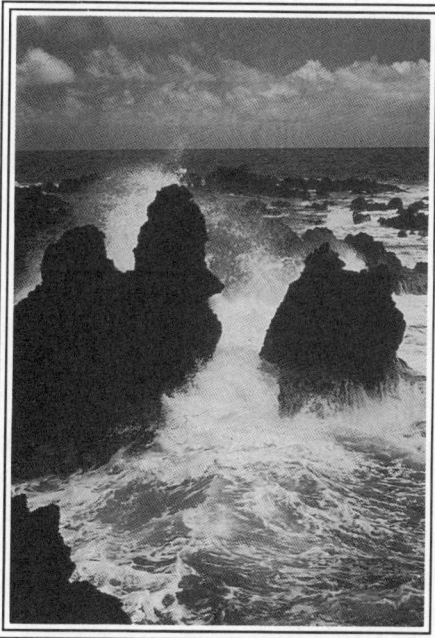

God is tossing our
Sins into the sea
And they are sinking
Never to be seen again.
Cute sins,
Ugly sins,
Stubborn sins,
Hasty sins,
Cruel sins,
Borderline sins,
Bawdy sins.

Sins are made of
Poor quality.
They do not float.
They do not resurface.
Divers will not find
Our sins.
Oceanographers
Will not uncover them
On some future
Expeditions.
Sins can be forgiven,
Cast into the sea,
And
Forgotten,
Never to rise again.

☞

"You will again have compassion on us;
  you will tread our sins underfoot and hurl
  all our iniquities into the depths of the sea."
Micah 7:19, NIV

AN APOLOGY TO GOD

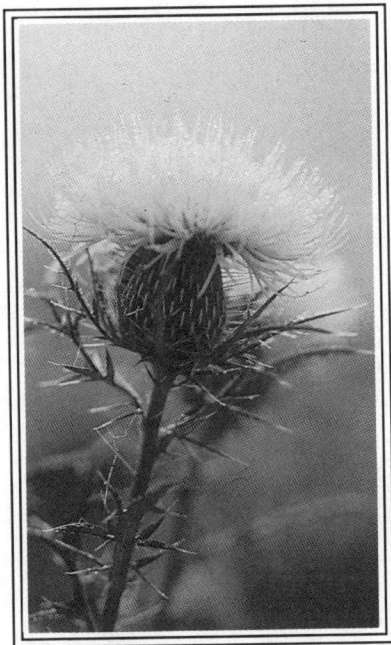

I tried hard to believe
That God brought everything
Into my life.

And for every falling leaf,
For every changing wind,
I looked for a purpose,
A hidden meaning,
Some secret code to
Give me direction.

If the price of spinach
Went down,
I thought it was a sign
That God wanted me
To start wolfing down
The green mess.

And if I got chapped lips,
God was telling me
I talked too much
And should give them
A rest.

With every piece of mail,
Behind every conversation
I wondered what God
Was up to.

Because of that, I blamed
God for each bit of
Misfortune.
For sleeplessness,
For stiffnecks,
For bills past due,
For dry skin
As well as acne.

But now I see
More clearly.

God is not bringing
Pain into my life
To teach me lessons.

God is taking pain
And making the best
Of it,
Giving reasons to go on,
Supplying hope for tomorrow.

I apologize for
Blaming God
For everything.

&

"And we know that in all things God works
for the good of those who love him,
who have been called according to his purpose."
Romans 8:28, NIV

LOOKING FOR HOPE

We have put our hope
In friends,
And it felt good
To know someone well,
To depend on them,
To share our ups and downs.

But friends move away,
Or friends die,
And you have to find
New ones.

We have put our hope
In things,
And we were happy
To have homes and boats,
Nice cars,
And a good job.

But prices dropped,
Plants closed,
And cars began
To rattle and rust.

We have put our hope
In youth.
And it felt great
To be able to do anything
And to be anywhere.

But our eyes dimmed,
Our teeth became plastic,
And our heart gave up
Its steady, measured beat.

We have put our hope
In God
And it felt terrific
To know
That He never went away,
Left us alone,
Or forgot where
He placed us.

When we lost hope
In the things we saw,
God still gave us hope
In what we have never seen.

And when everything
Seemed to fail,
God gave us hope.

&

"Find rest, O my soul, in God alone;
my hope comes from him."
Psalm 62:5, NIV

THE DARK SIDE

We want to be upbeat,
Positive optimists
Who reek with goodness.

We like to put forward
Our best foot
And talk about the best
In all of us.

And yet we know
Strong influences both
From the outside
And the inside
Push us toward
The dark side.

The dark side
Chooses to hate.
The dark side
Plots revenge.
The dark side
Wants to hurt.
The dark side
Seeks independence
From God.

As much as I
Change how I look,
As refined as I
Make my manners,
The dark side
Never goes away.

As educated as I become,
As well-read as I am,
It never goes away.

I must beware
Because the dark side
Presses in to
Control my life.

If I fail to check
My thoughts and attitudes
And what comes into my life,
The dark side will
Take over.

I visit with God
And ask Him to help
By the power that overcomes
The dark side.

And we work together
So the dark side
Won't gain control.

&

"But deliver us from the evil one."
Matthew 6:13, NIV

REMEMBER THE SPECIAL ONES

It's fun to flip the pages
In your mind,
To go through the mental album
Of the people who
Have meant so much.

To remember the young people
Who used to dunk you in the lake
On Saturday afternoons,
And hold hands and pray together
On Sunday nights.

To flash back and see the face
Of the college student who
Showed you how to live
Like a Christian
By his example
Without pushing or pulling.
It made you want to
Live like Christ
Because it seemed to look
So good
On your college friend.

To see again the Christian friend
You dated.
And the two of you wondered together
How God was working
In your lives.

To picture the pastor who
Lovingly taught and
Patiently listened and
Carefully guided and
Tenderly accepted you
For who you were.

It's fun to flip the pages
In your mind,
To go through the mental album
Of the people who
Have meant so much.

&

"I thank my God every time I remember you."
Philippians 1:3, NIV

LEANING ON
A SPIDER WEB

My friend had a farm
And he said to himself,
This is what life was
Meant to be.

The freedom of it all,
The open air and
The chance to make it
On my own.

Then a letter came
From the bank,
And a car came
From the sheriff,
And a team came
With the auctioneer,
And a truck came
To carry everything
Away.

My friend stood
By the fence
And looked across
An empty field
And thought to himself.

What can I count on,
Where can I go,
What can I lean on
That will not move
Or give way?

Is all of life
A spider web?
Weak and spindly,
Giving way
At the slightest touch?

He wondered.
He pondered.
He worried.

And my friend
Asked God to become
His immovable rock.

℘

"What he trusts in is fragile;
what he relies on is a spider's web."
Job 8:14, NIV

PROVERBS OF ASHES

Everyone knows what
You should do.
So they offer advice
Like palm readers
Or star gazers.

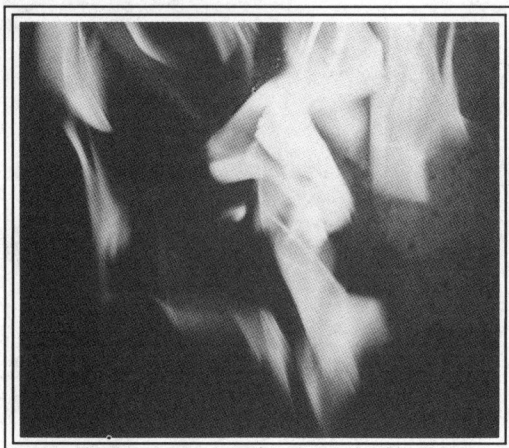

Plotting moves
For your life,
Divining formulas
For your dilemma,
Brewing remedies
For your ailments.

They may mean well,
And then again
They may want to
Just wiggle in.

They give advice
That often proves
To be no more
Than mere
Proverbs of ashes.

Burnt out wisdom.
Easy solutions.
Quick fixes.
Superficial answers.

Microwave wisdom.

Proverbs of ashes
That leave you
Dry
And tasteless.

> They may mean well,
> And then again
> They may want to
> Just wiggle in.
>
> They make you long
> For the friend
> Who comes to listen.
> ❦

"Your maxims are proverbs of ashes."
Job 13:12, NIV

NIGHT MONSTERS

Every now and then
When the sun goes away,
Our problems get together
And gang up on us.

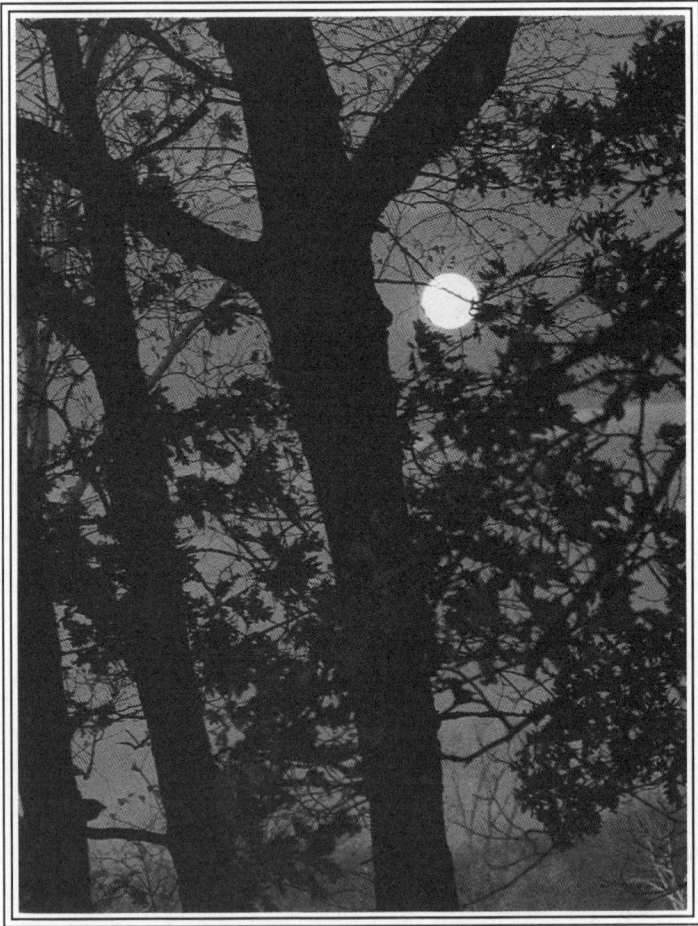

During the day we usually
Separate our problems
And fight them off
One by one.

But late at night
They're harder to see,
More difficult to identify,
Harder to pick out and handle.

Sneaking around
Through the shadows,
Cowards are
Waiting for us
To grow weak.

They then move
In an ugly group
And overwhelm us.

Come to our side,
O Lord,
In the darkness,
And stand between
The night monsters
And us.

Wrap us in your strength
When we have no strength
Of our own.

Our logic has turned
To sand.
Our defenses are like
Quicksilver.

Give us sleep
While you stay awake.
Give us peace
While you stand guard.

In the morning
We will find
New strength
For the battle.

&

"Night pierces my bones; my gnawing pains
never rest. In his great power God becomes
like clothing to me; he binds me like the
neck of my garment."
Job 30:17-18, NIV

THE WAY I AM

Could you reach out
And accept me
Just the way I am?

Complete with my
Strange attitude
And off-the-wall
Approach?

Can I survive
In your group
With my odd
Views
And a couple
Of quirks?

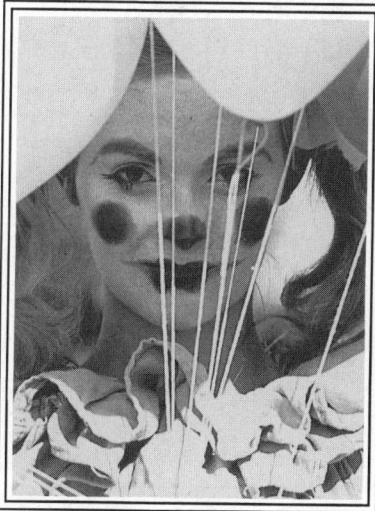

Would you tell me
To come back again
And really mean it
With your voice,
With your eyes,
And
With your heart?

Will you tolerate
My off-beat humor,
My questioning mind,
My shoes with
Argyle strings?

Dare you try
To appreciate me
For my differences
And encourage me
To stay that way?

> Will you look
> For Christ
> In me?
> And will you
> Accept me
> Because I
> Belong to Him?

> > Tell me I am
> > One with you
> > Just the way
> > I am.

> > Because we are
> > United in Jesus Christ.

> > &

"Accept one another, then,
just as Christ accepted you,
in order to bring praise to God."
Romans 15:7, NIV

NEVER THE SAME

They were like other Christians,
Good people, hard workers.
They drove trucks, wielded hammers,
Planted corn, sat behind desks.

Five people who believed,
Listened to sermons,
Watched slides and
Attended potlucks
And covered-dish dinners.

Balanced people who golfed,
Visited coffee shops,
And went fishing
Now and then.

Wholesome lives,
Solid people,
Good friends
Who had problems
Now and then.

Suddenly they took a challenge
To fly away for awhile
To dig wells and help others
In a far-off land.

They went
Like weekend missionaries
Just to dabble,
Help a bit
And have
A few laughs.

But they saw children
With bloated stomachs
And sunken eyes.

They saw children
Who would die
Because they had
No food or water,
Children who were
Being murdered
By tiny parasites
They could not see.

They stood by their sides
And watched pure water
Gush from a well
They helped dig.
And they cried.

They stood by their sides
And sang about Jesus
And His love.

And they will never
Be the same.

❦

"Suppose a brother or sister is without clothes
and daily food. If one of you says to him,
'Go, I wish you well; keep warm and well fed,'
but does nothing about his physical needs,
what good is it?"   James 2:15-16, NIV

BELIEVING ANYTHING

We are so eager
To believe that
We believe
Almost anything.

If a local prophet
Claims that the rise
In phone rates
Is a sign of
The second coming,
We cheer with joy.

And if we hear
A rumor of
Horses being massed
In Hawaii,
We merely nod
And say,
"I told you so."

Or to be told
That the word
"Camel" in Scripture
Always refers to
Kuwait
Sends us busily
Marking our Bibles.

We are so eager
To believe that
We believe
Almost anything.

℘

"A simple man believes anything."
Proverbs 14:15, NIV

A HUMBLE WARDROBE

Every fashion-conscious Christian knows
That pride is in vogue today.
We wear our talents on our sleeve
And don arrogance high
On our head.

We are the "king's kids."
We pad ourselves with possessions,
Collect trinkets because
God's children "deserve the best."

Self-assured, assertive, winners,
We have joined the flow
Of "upward mobility"
And run churches with
Young executives who can
Set goals and establish
Good marketing procedures
For God's work.

The mission of Christ
Is no longer
Second rate, shy or begging
For respect.

We are dressed in power,
Decked in opinion polls,
Tasseled in high ratings.

It's all impressive.
It's all amazing.
It's even refreshing
To a point.

But maybe we are
Making a mistake
In giving our sandals
Away.

Maybe we have lost
The quiet dignity of
Humility.

Where are the garments
Of servitude,
Of tenderness,
Of gratitude,
Of sharing?

Have we shed those
For the expensive cloth
Of power?

"Clothe yourselves with humility toward
one another, because, 'God opposes the proud
but gives grace to the humble.'"
1 Peter 5:5, NIV

THE CHURCH ALIVE

A friend shook my hand / And smiled at me like
I had lowered gas prices.

Another friend hugged me / And said how much
He missed me when / I was away.

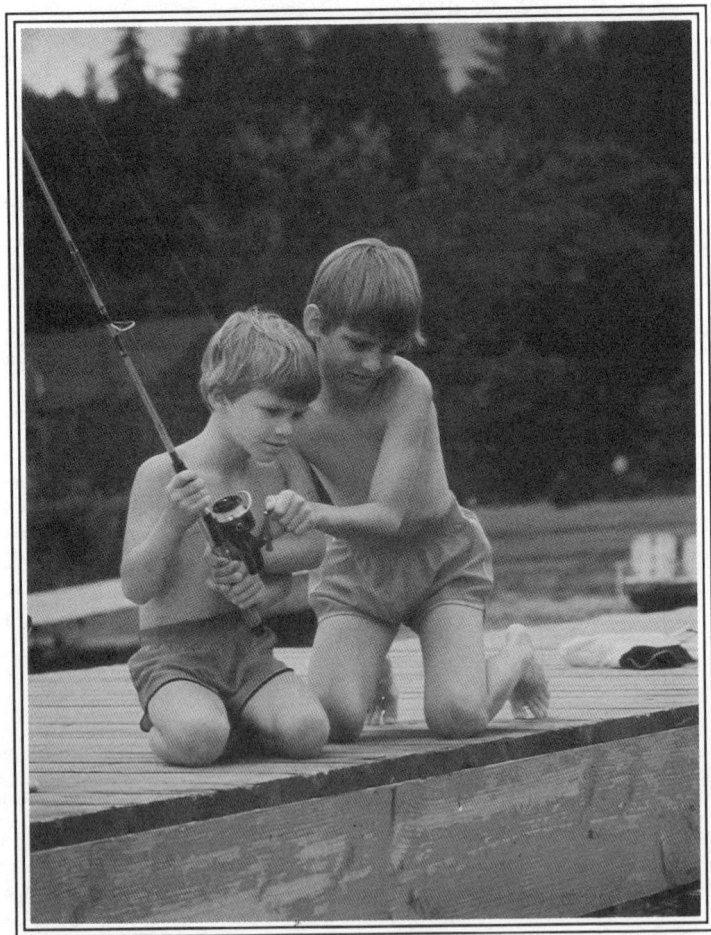

They passed a plate
For a man who
Had his electricity
Turned off.

Then they rose as one
And sang about God
And told Him how much
He meant in their lives.

We sat for a while
And heard what God
Was like,
And what He could do
For our lives
And for others.

As we inched our way
Toward the door,
A man stopped us to ask
If he could help Saturday
When we moved the branches
From our backyard.

The Church of Jesus Christ
Was alive.

&

"All believers were together
and had everything in common."
Acts 2:44, NIV

THE GREAT CAMPER

Walking your children
To the lake,
To swim and dig
Tunnels in the sand.

Passing tents,
Campers,
R.V.'s.

Watching fathers thread
The fishing gear
And children search
For wood.
Seeing mothers hang
Dishcloths on
Makeshift clotheslines.

The rich and the poor,
The young and the old
All mixed together to share
The out-of-doors,
The cool breezes,
And burned marshmallows
Sprinkled with sand.

And you remember
The Great Camper,
Jesus Christ.

The verse says
(in the original of course)
That the Word
Pitched His tent
Among us.

He came down to do
What we do.
He came to feel
What we feel.

You catch yourself,
Just for a second,
Looking around.

Could He be
Here now?

Would Jesus be
Adjusting snorkel equipment,
Cooking hot dogs on the grill,
Or hitting fly balls
In the field?

He came to be
One of us
In the flesh,
Pitching His tent
Among us.

&

"The Word became flesh
and lived for a while among us."
John 1:14, NIV

PRACTICE LEAPING

It's hard to keep up
With everything that
Is required of me.

But I have tried
To keep all that
Is asked.

I even bought a Bible
With four translations
To make sure I didn't
Miss any commands.

Anxious to collect
Every conceivable blessing,
I have starved my soul,
Fed my soul,
Packed my soul,
Had it reconstituted
And once reshuffled.

However, only recently
I have discovered
The theology of
Leaping.

It's true!
The Bible tells me
To leap for joy.

No normal complainer,
I do see
Considerable risk
With this neglected
Expression of faith.

Leaving the ground
At my age, size,
And poor equilibrium
Is to tempt
Serious injury.

Not too sure how high
I can get into space,
The launch is only
Part of the problem.

Landing, while doubtless
Healthy for my soul,
Could bring permanent
Damage to my body.

But never question
My dedication.
The next time
I feel overcome
With joy,
I promise to
Stand on a
Footstool
And leap to
The floor.

I can only hope
That I am not
Flooded with joy
Too often.

&

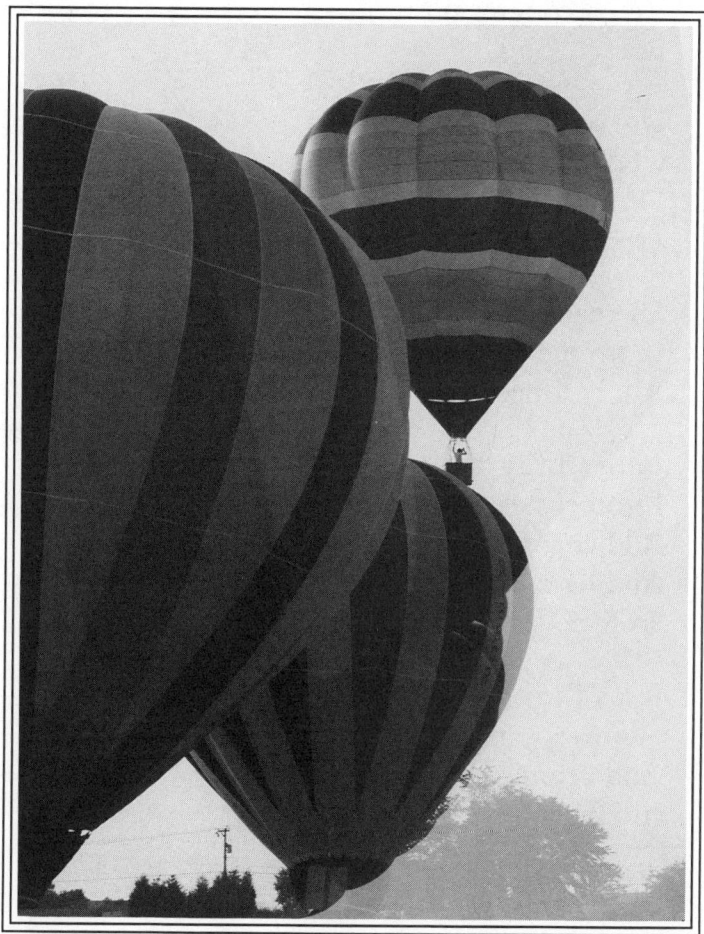

"Leap for joy."
Luke 6:23, NIV

A CHANGED LIFE

Yesterday a woman
Gave her testimony
In church
And a congregation
Praised God.

Not a light testimony.
God had not delivered her
From blue suede shoes or
From excessive bowling.

She had not been rescued
From the edge of
A life of needlepoint.

Jesus Christ had reached
Into her heart
And changed her life,
And had given her a reason
To live.

Jesus Christ had told her
She was valuable
And promised her a place
In His family.

It had been a year
Since she first met
Christ
And He had proved
Faithful.

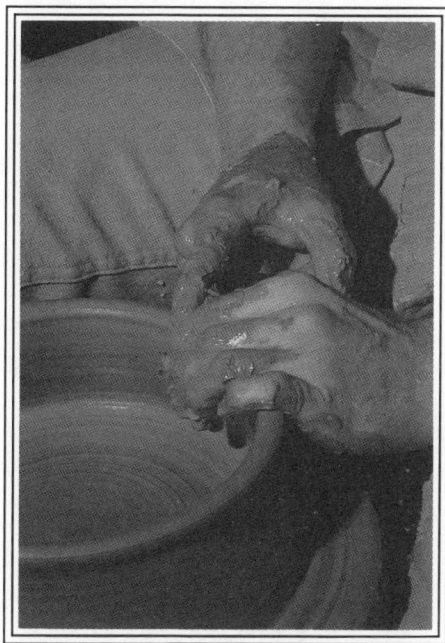

Yesterday a woman
Gave her testimony
In church
And a congregation
Praised God.

℘

IF GOD GIVES MERCY

If God gives mercy
And abounds with grace,
Why can't we forgive ourselves?

If God accepts us
And is liberal with forgiveness,
Why are we so harsh
And angry with ourselves?

God holds us beneath
His wings
While we hold ourselves
Under the whip.

God supplies encouragement.
Why then would we supply
Discouragement?

If God smiles at us,
Why do we frown at
Ourselves?

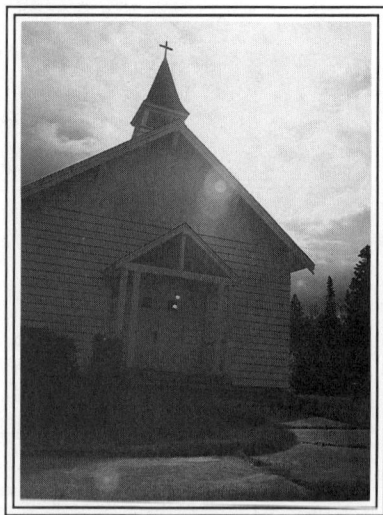

If God treats us as
Family,
Why do we treat ourselves as
Strangers?

If God gives mercy
And abounds with grace,
Why can't we forgive ourselves?

God calls us friends
While we call ourselves
Enemies.

God gives us understanding.
Why do we give ourselves
Coldness?

If God loves us,
Why do we call ourselves
Ugly?

If God is longsuffering,
Why are we impatient
With ourselves?

If God gives us mercy,
Could we not give ourselves
Mercy, too?

❧

"Blessed are the merciful."
Matthew 5:7, NIV

NAILING IT DOWN

Everything in life
Seems to change.
Hairlines recede.
Waistlines expand.

Our friends look older
And college students
Seem to grow younger
Every year.

We fight a nation
One year
And then defend
The same government
The next.

Everything in life
Seems to change.
Some changes are
Good
And others are
Terrible.

But too much change,
Constant change,
Makes us confused,
Afraid and bewildered.

Fortunately some things
Never change.
God has driven
Some large nails
Into some huge
Beams.

The nails God has
Driven
Do not change
With each fad
Or fade
With each trend.

God's nails are
Immovable.
God's nails are
Dependable.

And we can
Hang our coats
On them.

&

"The words of the wise are like goads,
  their collected sayings like firmly
  embedded nails — given by one Shepherd."
  Ecclesiastes 12:11, NIV

DOES GOD LIKE US?

Could it be that God
Does more than just
Love us?

We make it sound like
God puts up with us.
He tolerates, provides,
Forgives, even creates,
But in fact doesn't care much
For us personally.

As if
God can barely tolerate
Being around us.

It sounds good to insist
That we are nothing,
That we have little
To offer,
As if God would be
Totally bored with any
Of our meanderings.

But how can any
Relationship exist
Where one person
Holds the other
With contempt?

Such cannot be.

God enjoys talking
To us,
Not merely to teach
Or to wax eloquent.

God likes to hear
From us
Because He is
A good listener.

He wants to know
About our dreams,
Our plans and
Our children.

He wants to know
What we want.
Jesus taught us that.

Maybe God does not only
Love us,
Though that would be
Plenty.

Maybe, just maybe,
God also likes us,
Even if we do not care
Much for ourselves.

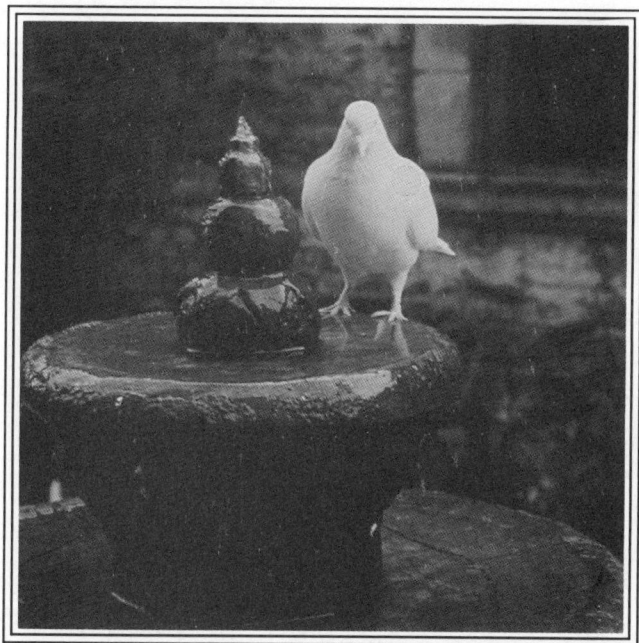

Practice saying it to
Ourselves,
Slowly at first,
For it may sound
Strange.

God likes us
And enjoys
Our fellowship.

℘

"We proclaim to you what we have
seen and heard, so that you also may have
fellowship with us. And our fellowship is
with the Father and with his Son, Jesus Christ."
1 John 1:3, NIV

WHEN GOD WHISTLES

If God wants something done,
All He has to do is pucker up / And whistle.
Storms will come racing in / Or go roaring out
Merely because God gave / The signal.

If God needs an invasion / Of bees,
He simply puts two fingers / In His mouth
And whistles for them to / Show up.

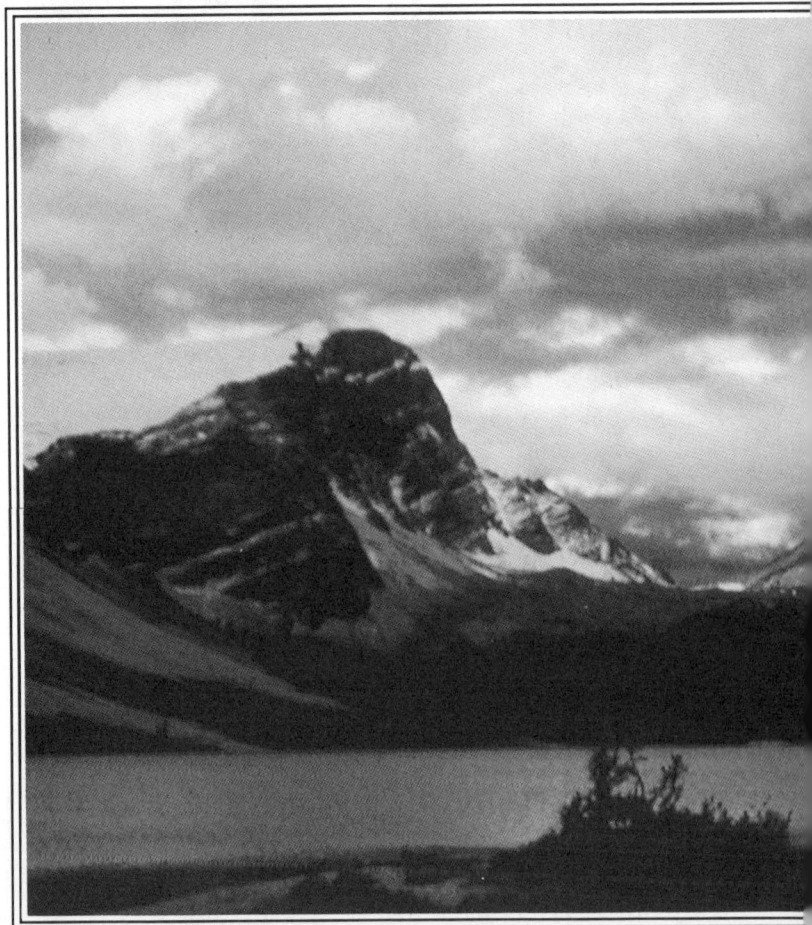

Nature has a great respect / For God,
And even its simplest forms / Would obey if
God called.

As Christians, / As followers, / As believers,
As disciples / We listen for
That same whistle.

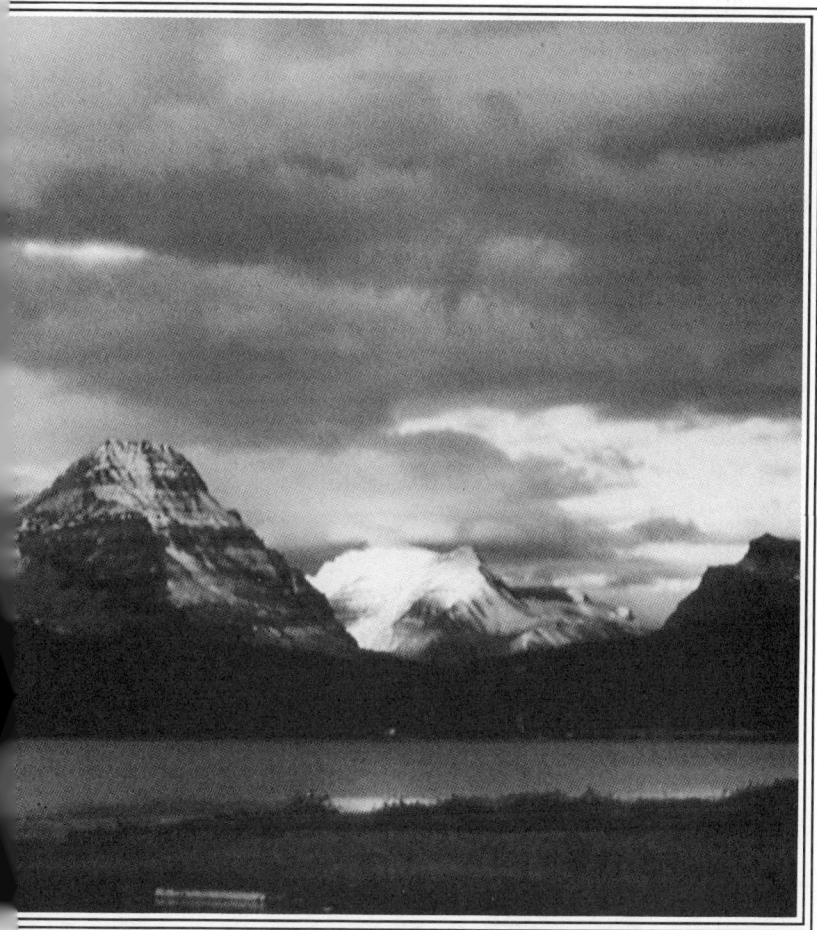

Does God want
The hungry fed?
Does God ask that
Babies be saved?
All He has to do
Is pucker up
And whistle.

Does God want
The good news
Shared
And the love
Of Christ
Presented?

Does God want
The desperate
Calmed and encouraged?
The elderly and sad
Cheered?

All He has to do
Is pucker up
And whistle.

Christians listen carefully
For the whistle
From God.

&

"In that day the Lord will whistle
for flies from the distant streams of Egypt
and for bees from the land of Assyria."
Isaiah 7:18, NIV

TO FOSSILIZE

We discussed contemporary music
While Haitians starved,
Alcoholics died in the streets,
And children were abused.

We argued over facial hair
While the homeless
Slept in alleys,
Teenagers ran away,
And fathers shot themselves.

We debated over communion wafers
While mothers aborted
In heatless apartments,
Indians stared in gloom,
And millions of Africans
Never heard of Christ.

We pondered over fine doctrine
While racial hatred ruled,
Men perished in prison,
And the penniless died
From diseases for which
There are cures.

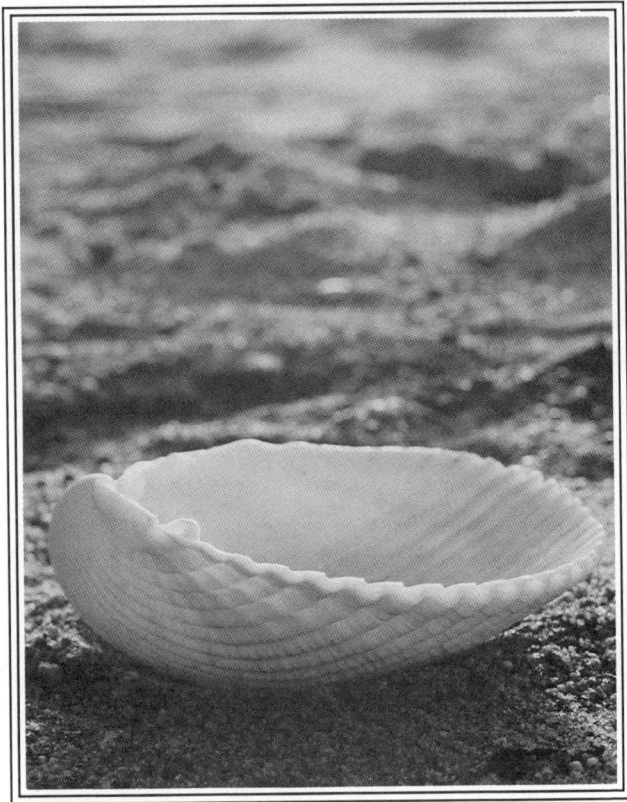

Some talk,
Others go.
Some worry,
Others work.
Some curse,
Others heal.
Some fossilize,
Others mobilize.

℘

"But someone will say, 'You have
faith; I have deeds.' Show me your faith
without deeds, and I will show you my faith
by what I do."

James 2:18, NIV

ROOM FOR THE FLOPPY

We wish we
Had it all together,
But we don't.

We are floppy Christians.
We are poorly disciplined,
Have trouble being on time,
Have a garbage bag
Full of bad habits.

But we like to think
God loves floppy Christians.

We read the Bible
In fits and starts.
We don't memorize
Bible verses because
We forget where
We put the packet.

Not unlike insects,
We wiggle out
For a short season,
Work hard for Christ,
And then retreat
Before the cold winds
Catch us.

It isn't that we
Don't believe.
It isn't that we
Don't care.
It isn't even that
We don't love.
We are just
Floppy Christians.

We have been adequately
Taught,
Admonished,
Encouraged,
Threatened,
Cajoled,
Prodded and
Goaded
About the values of
The disciplined life.

We even concede the fact
That people who have it
All together just might
Get more done.

But that doesn't change us.
We are the rumpled shirts
Of Christianity.
Wrinkled and worn,
Tossed on the back
Of a chair.

The disciplined life
Is the good life,
But it's not our life.

But we like to think
God loves floppy Christians.

I couldn't find the verse that goes
with this thought. Then I got tired
of looking for it.
Bill Coleman

CHECK THE CRACKS

Solomon is universally saluted
As one of the wisest men
To ever stick his brainy head
Above the crowd.

Smart enough to keep his nation
At peace,
Clever enough to collect mounds
Of gold,
Sharp enough to become one of
The world's most famous judges.

Granted, his armor showed a bit
Of rust
When he gathered female companions,
Like a third grader lining up
Bottle caps.

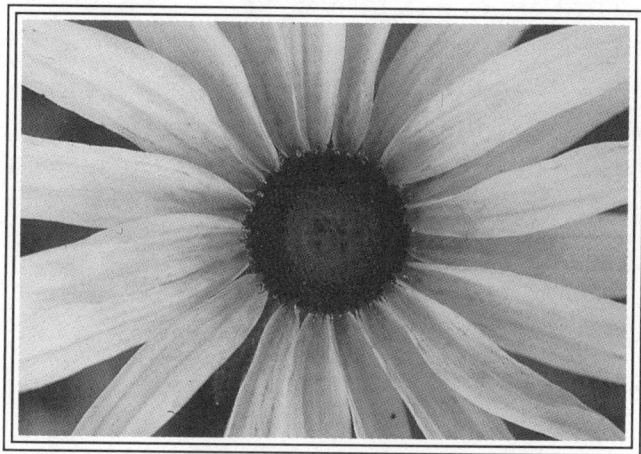

But, all in all, the picture holds
Intact.
God blessed Solomon,
Protected him,
And gave him enough wisdom
To keep peace in the Middle East.

Between running a government,
Holding court,
And carrying out the trash
For hundreds of women,
Solomon must have been
A busy executive.

Yet, Solomon had enough sense
To take time out
And look at God's
Creation.

He checked out the lizards,
Watched eagles lock their wings
And sail across the sky,
Took notes on the deer
Darting over the fields
And stopping to sniff
The wind.

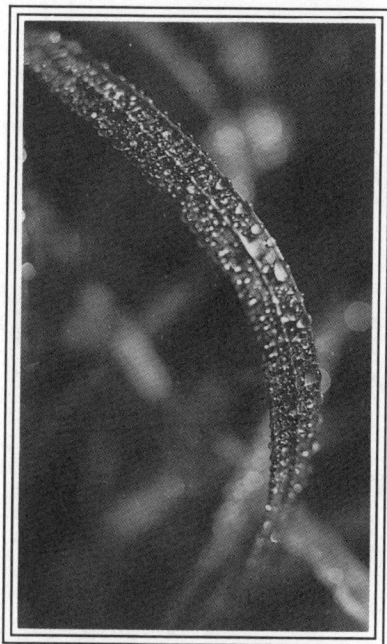

We can imagine Solomon
Sitting early on the dew-damp
Grass,
Turban pushed back off his
Forehead,
Hoping to see a fox pausing
On a log in the distance.

To see him sprawled out flat
On his stomach
Studying God's little creatures
Crawling in the cracks
Along the road,
Or pasted against a wall
Looking for new life forms.

A wise, godly king
Wise enough to slow down
And check the cracks.
Godly enough to worship
The Creator who made
The real wonders of
This world.

❦

"He described plant life, from the cedar of Lebanon
to the hyssop that grows out of walls. He also taught
about animals and birds, reptiles and fish."
1 Kings 4:33, NIV

MEASURING UP

When we were adolescents,
We spent most of
Our waking hours
Comparing ourselves
With everyone else.

> "Are we as tall?"
> Turned into
> "Are we as strong?"

>> "Are we as smart?"
>> Turned into
>> "Are we as pretty?"

We all played it,
Because we wanted
To know,
Because we needed
To know
How we measured up.

By comparing ourselves
With everyone else,
We tried to find out
Who we were,
What we were,
Because we were looking
To see
How valuable we were.

Those were the adolescent years —
The awkward, ugly, gangly
Years of insecurity,
Years of immaturity.

We became older,
Smarter, braver.
We have learned
To be content
With what we are,
And what God
Has made us.

Haven't we?

&

"For I have learned to be content
whatever the circumstances."
Philippians 4:11, NIV

TOUGH DAYS

Some days are tougher
Than others.
Cakes drop instead of rise.
Paint runs instead of dries.
And even the vultures
Can't find a carcass.

You'd catch a train and
Run away,
But trains don't run
On time.

Some days are tougher
Than others.
Your belt is in its last notch,
You lost your car keys,
And junior spilled cereal
On your report.

You would quit your job
In a huff,
But the boss got sick
And didn't come in.

Some days are tougher
Than others.
You got a bill for cat food
And you don't own a cat.
The Latin Club Mothers
Want you to bake brownies
For 128.
And you found a "magazine"
Under your son's pillow.

You want to resign
From the human race,
But you can't find anyone
To accept your resignation.

Fortunately, every day has
An end
And every morning has
A beginning.

Each morning brings its own hope.
Each dawn offers a new life.
Each sunrise invites us to start
All over again.

Every day God greets us
At the bathroom mirror
And says,
"Let's start all over again."

&

"Weeping may remain for a night,
but rejoicing comes in the morning."
Psalm 30:5, NIV

SLAMMED THE DOOR

She thought she left
Her pain behind
When she slammed the door.

She walked away
With head held high,
And looked for tomorrow
Without him.

It was a bad marriage,
A bad mix.
Too many tears
And no way to
Work it out.
So she slammed the door.

How was she to know
What lawyers' fees would be?
How was she to know
That support checks
Wouldn't come?
How was she to know
She would cry alone?
How was she to know
Her child would feel the hurt?

It looked so easy.
She saw it
A hundred times
On television.
A few angry words,
A hurried suitcase
And soon everything
Was fine.

But life isn't television.
People are real
Who dare to feel,
And the pain runs
Deep.

Life's problems are
Not settled,
They are not
Eased
By the slamming
Of doors.

She wishes someone
Had told her.
She wishes she
Had listened
Before she slammed
The door.

&

"Therefore what God has joined together,
let man not separate."
Matthew 19:6, NIV

HELD HOSTAGE

I pledge to myself
That I will not
Be held hostage by
Hating someone else.

If I hate someone,
The person I hate
Controls my behavior.

They make my stomach
Acids flow.
They increase my blood
Pressure
To geyser hot.

They cause me to
Say things that are
Hurtful, mean, and
Belittling.

They make me avoid
Some places and
Some situations.

They shrink my soul.
They shrivel my spirit.
They diminish my
Potential
To serve God.

They limit my ability
To love those who
Are close.

To release myself,
All I need to do
Is forgive them.

Through forgiveness,
I am delivered
And I can walk
Away.

As long as I hate
That person,
We are locked together
In a life and death
Struggle.

Neither of us dare
Relax or give in.

In one wide sweep
I set myself free.
I merely forgive him.

&

"But I tell you who hear me:
Love your enemies, do good
to those who hate you."
Jesus Christ—Luke 6:27, NIV

ANGELS IN RAGS

Who are the hungry
Who search for food
In garbage pails
In alleys behind
Plush restaurants?

Who are the poor
Who are dressed
In shreds,
With children cuddled
Close to their feet?

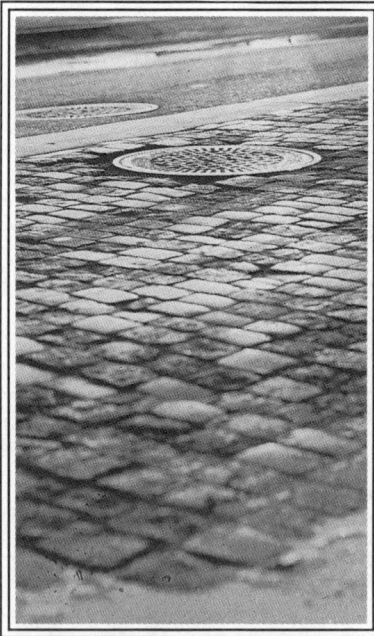

Who are the homeless
Who sleep on heat vents
And prop cardboard boxes
To their backs
To hold out
The night winds?

Who are the sick
Who lose their sight,
Or drag their feet,
Or fail to read
In Calcutta
And Chicago?

Who are the hopeless
Who cannot think,
But hold on to life
Through despair
As long as they dare?

Who are the lonely
Trapped within themselves,
Held by invisible locks,
Afraid to venture into
A world God created?

Are they losers?
Are they useless?
Are they clowns
To be laughed at,
Despised and rejected?

Are they castoffs
Who missed life's boat
And are ridiculed
For their loss?

Some may be angels
Sent by God,
Waiting for our love.
Some may be angels
Dressed in rags,
Waiting for our love.

&

"He who mocks the poor shows
contempt for their Maker."
Proverbs 17:5, NIV

THE ANSWER MAN

In the early days
When we first found
Christ,
Or Christ found us,
Or whatever,
We had the answers
To everything.

We knew left from right,
Black from white,
Up from down and
Every shade of difference.

Just ask us,
Spell out the problem;
We had the answer.

We could turn to
The page,
Quote the speaker,
Or rehash the cliché
As we heard it
A thousand times.

We could tell others
What was best for them
And how to put
Their life in order.

We were that way.
But we grew
And we learned
And we hurt
And we cried
And we found
Life wasn't
So simple.

Finally, but painfully,
We retired Mr. Answer Man
And became servants
And guides for others.

We became less authorities
And more searchers.
We became less judges
And more fellow pilgrims.

We became slower
To condemn,
Slower to denounce.
We became better
At listening,
At sharing,
At feeling.

God has done a job
At slaying
Mr. Answer Man.

&

"You, then, why do you judge your brother?
Or why do you look down on your brother?
For we will all stand before God's judgment seat."
Romans 14:10, NIV

WALKING MY GOAT

Every few days I get the urge
To load up my goat
And take him for a walk.

Walking my goat is one of
My favorite pastimes.
I load him up heavy,
Pack him down tight
And double check the ropes.

I stack my problems on him
One at a time.
I include a pile of my bad habits,
A sack of my moodiness,
A crate load of my grouchiness,
Two duffle bags of self-pity,
One box of flakiness and
A bottle of selfishness.

Fully loaded, my goat follows.
Stiff-legged, sway-backed,
Head drooping, he takes each step
Deliberately, painfully
Under the terrible strain.

I'm walking my scapegoat.
I want him to take the blame
For all my problems, light and heavy,
Short and tall, old and new.

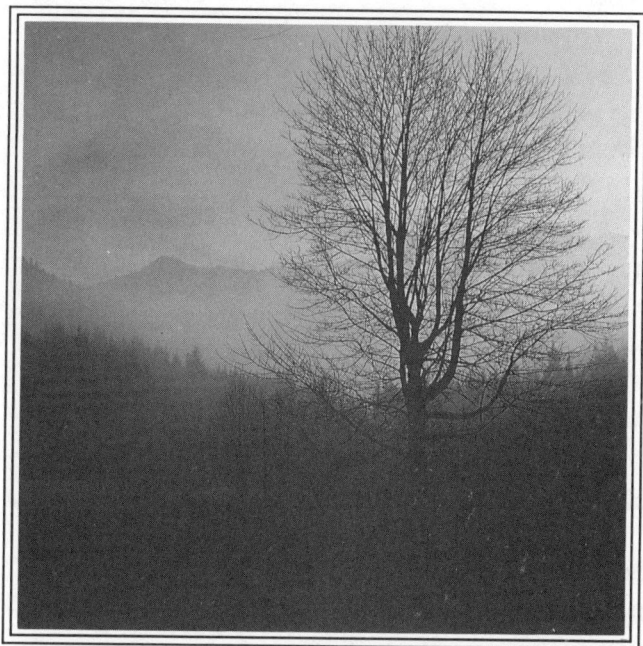

And when we have walked far
Out into the country,
I tie my goat to a tree
And I walk back home.

For a couple of hours
I'm happy, content
In my dream world.

My problems are gone,
And that's only fair.
After all, they weren't
Really mine anyway.

They were caused by my parents.
They were caused by my spouse.
They were invented by my boss.
They were forged by my children.
They were imagined by my doctor.
They were forced by my minister.

For those few hours I live
In a fairyland,
Dreaming that my problems
Belong to someone else.

Then I look in the yard,
And almost on schedule
I see my goat standing
By the magnolias.

Worn-out, tired from the trip,
He stands there stubbornly
Waiting to be unloaded.

So I go and begin to untie
The awkward burden.
My problems are my problems.
I will have to handle them.
Making others my scapegoat
Never seems to work.

I'll handle, shuffle, process,
File, store, and deal
With my problems
Like an adult,
At least for a while.

But in a couple of weeks,
Maybe a month,
I'll feel overloaded again.
And when I do, I'll load up
My goat and take him
For a walk.

And my goat will
Stay away
For a little while
Before it brings them all back
Home.

My sins are my sins.
I must own up
To them,
For no scapegoat
Can haul them away.

&

"Then I acknowledged my sin to you
and did not cover up my iniquity.
I said, 'I will confess my transgressions to the Lord' —
and you forgave the guilt of my sin."
Psalm 32:5, NIV

THE SIMPLE FORMULA

What does God want
From us?
When will He be pleased
With us?
What standard has God set
For us?

Ask a dozen people;
Get a dozen answers.

Read a dozen books;
Find a dozen formulas.

Hear a dozen speakers;
Know a dozen ways.

Could it be so simple,
Would it be so clear
That God wants us to
Love the Lord our God
And also to
Love our neighbor as ourselves?

Look out for the protests.
There is more to it
Than that.
That's good but it's only
A start.
Remember to include the
Entire Bible.

Count the objections.
Listen to the clauses,
The "buts" and "howevers"
And "furthermores."

Like theo-lawyers we
Argue for exceptions,
Extenuating circumstances,
And suppression of evidence.

> But Jesus did say it,
> Didn't He?
> Before there were organizations,
> And printing presses,
> And spiritual formulas,
> And dazzling seminars,
> And overhead projectors,
> And video-cassettes.
> Jesus did say it,
> Didn't He?
>
> Before there were huge budgets,
> Professional fund raisers,
> Direct mailing lists,
> And corporation jets,
> Jesus did say it,
> Didn't He?

To love the Lord our God
And also to
Love our neighbors as ourselves.
The formula is so simple.

℘

"'Love the Lord your God with all your heart and with
all your soul and with all your strength and with all
your mind'; and, 'Love your neighbor as yourself.'"
Luke 10:27, NIV

❧ BEING DIFFERENT

She didn't dress
The way they did,
Not because she couldn't,
But because
She didn't want to.

She didn't attend everything
The way they did.
She picked and chose
What she felt fit
Her mix.

She didn't always shake
Her head
The way they did.
Half the time
Her head nodded "yes"
While theirs shook "no,"
And then
Just the opposite.

She didn't see every
Bible verse
The way they did.
She questioned, speculated,
And wondered out loud.
She said, "What if…"
And "I'm not sure."

But she smiled
And hugged them
And spoke of Christ
And tried to follow
And learn to sacrifice.

And they loved her
For all of her
Differences.

℘

"One man's faith allows him to eat everything,
but another man, whose faith is weak,
eats only vegetables."

Romans 14:2, NIV

BUYING LOVE

An evangelist explained
How we could buy his love.

For dollars we could become
Part of his team,
Added to his list,
Kept informed,
And receive enough mail
To fill a dump truck.

Cash would make us part
Of his inner-circle.
No other qualifications
Were necessary.
He didn't care if we had
The personality of an
Electric sander.
He didn't ask if we had
Membership in subversive groups.
Just send the cash.
Cash would make us part
Of his inner-circle.

Help him build vacation lands
And he will send us toy shovels
With "Jesus Loves Me" on the handles.

If we don't send cash,
God will go into a blue funk.
Apparently, God was counting on
A Christian entertainment center
Where His children could frolic
Together.

It doesn't sound like
A bad deal.
We don't have to become
Involved.
Just a check,
Even a credit card number.
If we send it now,
The speaker will thank God
For us
And he will personally
Love us.

It takes love back
To the cheap, cash-and-carry level,
The same as on the
Streets.

Thank God for free love
That reaches out to sinners
And does not depend on
Cash.

&

"But God demonstrates his own love for us in this:
While we were still sinners, Christ died for us."
Romans 5:8, NIV